Red Letter Openings

The Poetry Society of the Open University

40th Anniversary Anthology

of

OU Poets

2021

Published 2021 by Open University Poets.

ISBN 978-1-7399361-0-5

Editor: Sue Spiers
Cover: Julie Anne Gilligan

Printed by Lulu.com

Lulu

About OUPS

OU Poets is the Poetry Society of the Open University. It is open to any student or staff member, past or present. At the time of going to press there are about 80 members from all over the U.K. with some in mainland Europe and worldwide.

Members of the society submit poems to a magazine, which is produced 5 times a year, each one having a different voluntary editor. The magazine is not a publication *per se* and is strictly produced by the members for the members. There is a section for comment and criticism of members' work.

At the end of the year, members are asked to vote for the 20 poems they most appreciated from the 5 magazines produced that year. Those with the most votes, allowing for no more than one poem per poet, appear in the following year's issue of Openings. The anthology is as broad-based as the society itself and reflects the varied backgrounds, interests and tastes of the members.

If you would like more information about OU Poets, please contact the Secretary:
>Kimberley Pulling
>secretary@oupoets.org.uk

or the Chair:
>Polly Stretton
>chair@oupoets.org.uk
>Tel: (+44) 1886 830054 for postal address information.

Or visit our website at http://www.oupoets.org.uk

 @OUPoets

Foreword from the Activities Officer

When I first noticed that 2021 was the 40th Anniversary of the founding of The Open University Poetry Society (OUPS), I immediately thought 'Anthology' as a way of celebrating not only the Society but also the members who have put so much time and effort into keeping it all going. As an alumna myself, I thought the theme could be around 'my personal journey: poetry and the OU'. I am delighted with the response from members old and new and the resulting book is one of which the members can be proud. A big thank you also goes out to all the OU tutors who have inspired and encouraged our poetic development. Enjoy!

Julie Anne Gilligan

Introduction

It's been a pleasure pulling this introduction together. Here is a fascinating insight into how our Society was established and grew. The form the introduction should take was quite a challenge initially, but the method was resolved when three founder members sent memories of the early days of OUP. Their reflections follow, with an overview from Archivist Phil Craddock.

Shirley Bell was the brains behind the Open University Poetry Society. She advertised in the OU "Sesame" magazine with a suggestion for forming the society. Wanting to share the work, three editors were nominated and took turns producing the new society's magazine. Shirley put the first issue together on a primitive duplicator.

Ted Griffin was one of the first to reply to Shirley. Ted says he had ambitions to be the first elected chairman when the opening annual meeting was held in Oxford but was beaten to it by Rodney Wood. 'I had the honour of becoming the second chairman of the Open University Poets.'

Ted continued, 'The early days were fraught with discussions that sometimes became a little heated. We early members took our poetry very seriously indeed'. The members decided that a magazine would unite them, but it took longer to select a format. Some thought a judging panel should decide on 'the best' poems to include, others, including Ted, thought that would be the kiss of death for the fledgling society. In the end, it was decided that every member must have the right to have poems in the magazine, a rule that still continues.

The early mags were wholly produced by the editor and varied from lavish to primitive. Ted recalls that the first one he produced involved him typing every poem then running it off on a Gestetner duplicating machine and stapling the pages together. He was greatly relieved when the Open University took on the production and distribution.

Ted became chairman after three years and says that some things were still undecided, particularly the number of magazines each year, which was erratic. 'During its 40 years, the magazine has given light to many good poems, some even great. It has been useful to would-be poets in allowing them to assess their work alongside others and thus, I believe, done a great service to the great English art of poetry which is so often the most neglected of the arts. I have always been proud of the society, and proud to be a member of such a distinguished organisation. Forty years! Wow!'

Jim Lindop attended an OU Summer School at the University of East Anglia in 1980. The course was TAD292 "Art and the Environment". 'I was,' Jim told us, 'at the age of 38, to become a poet.' He continued, 'Also attending that Summer School was a young man wearing a T-shirt that proclaimed, 'I AM A POEM'. His name was – and still is – Rodney Wood. Together, we signed up to be under the tutorship of Bill Billings, artist and poet, and he it was who kindled the feeling in me that I could be a poet, too. A few months later, an advertisement, placed in the OU Student Magazine "Sesame" by Shirley Bell, sought parties who might be interested in forming the Open University Poetry Society. Both Rodney and I replied, it was the first outlet for my nascent verse. We became founder members of this society. Now we are 40 and the Society is well-established and can boast a lively, talented membership. Here's to us!'

Phil Craddock reports that Shirley wrote to each new member laying out the aims of the society, all of which are still largely in place. In that first year, six workshop magazines were typed, replicated, and distributed by the membership, which was fifty-strong by June.

Phil says that Daphne Phillips, Ted Griffin and Jim Lindop have the distinction of being the only poets who have remained members of the Society from its creation at the beginning of 1981. John Starbuck and Hilary Mellon have been with the society the next longest, John joining late 1981 and Hilary in 1982.

'By October 1981 a constitution had been written and a Committee formed. The first Annual General Meeting was held in Oxford in April 1982, at which Rodney Wood became the first Chair. Later in 1982 Moira Andrew organised the very first November Weekend (which was actually at the end of October that year!) at the Arvon Centre, Totleigh Barton, in Devon, with Wes Magee as tutor.

'In 1983, the first OUP anthology was produced, called "Your Attention Please". In 1984 John Starbuck came up with the name "Openings", which we have used ever since. Daphne Phillips became Treasurer in 1983, Hilary Mellon the Activities Officer in 1984; both Ted and Jim were to be future holders of the Chair.

'The first forty years of the OUP had begun.'

What a treat to have such wonderful memories shared with us as an introduction to our 40th Anniversary Anthology. Many thanks to Shirley, Ted, Jim and Phil. This book celebrates the Society's first forty years. We hope you will enjoy reading it as much as we have enjoyed compiling it and indeed living it.

Contents

Contents

Denis Ahern

A Rhymester Reappraises

On my poetry shelf they stood,
those volumes gathered over time,
an orderly arboretum,
ballads, lyrics, rhythm and rhyme,
R J Simms's sad solemn willows,
Robert Service's tall straight pines.
No mystery or obscurity
you got what it said in each line.

And I wrote in that mode, juggling words,
       struggling with meter, imposing rigid form,
Although aware of those untamed Whitman lines,
       rambling wildly, verdantly leaved tendrils,
       undisciplined, defiant of topiary.
And I'd noticed those haikus – bonsai in extremis –
       impressive but prompting the question, 'Where's
       the rest of it?'

Then on the road to hoped-for enlightenment
I found an avenue, kaleidoscopically lined,
Holly, cactus, yucca mingled with oak, hornbeam,
       gooseberry bush, the occasional willow and pine.

The creators and appreciators of this diversity,
       a freewheelingly scholarly clan, drew me in,
       prompted an eye de-scaling.
And a voice whispered,
       'It's poetry, lad, not eleven times tables.'

My writing reappraised, knee-jerk formulations are gone.
Thesaurus and rhyming dictionary,
     secateurs, grafting knife and tape are set aside.
And my shelf – now a library – has become rain forest,
     tropical jungle, olive grove, furze covered heath.

Jane Avery

the load forsaken

new codes emerged as I knew they would
and wearied by TMA's and growth
yet eager to be understood
I wondered what is the likelihood
my poetry would be good enough

it was a rather sad affair
this craving to understand the game
applause for an essay or poetry where
blows arrive with surprising flair
a thorn then freely all out acclaim

an oath a dawning evenly play
at thieves launching a maniac
slow it crept accursed by some other way
bestowing byways deeds gone astray
redoubted awry another drawback

well now I'm sharing this by and by
threadbare but for the common sense
of those who urge to make good thereby
you OU poets clarified
and that has made this experience

Pru Bankes Price

Misconception of a Pair of Shoes

Whatever possessed me
on that derelict plateau
the wild urge of freedom

like a careless mother
abandons her babies
shoved those beauties
beneath midnight rocks
amongst debris of years
chaos of convention
to dance barefoot beneath
forgiving stars   a narrow moon

a year on   alert to the craving
delight of the dance calls me back
through shambles of brambles
keen for kick-back heels

one has surfaced tapping a toe
how so   where's the other
the identical twin
the mate   co-respondent
there should always be two
equals and even
today only half
right with no left
          the left lies distorted
          sleeps everlasting
          discarded   disregarded

but the right's proved a fighter
a delighter   a bouncer back
a hopper   trit-trotter
no regretter   it's better
to dance unrestrained
for the stallers   the fallers
    who never made it
    through conception
        to celebrate a half life
        preferred over no life at all

K. J. Barrett

The Spark that Lit the Fire

Every fire needs a spark,
"Season of mists and mellow fruitfulness",
Voices moving through me
Speaking to paper and pen.

Students full of jive,
Caribbean rhythms casting their spell,
Words spreading wings
On humming bird mornings,
Dull roots stirring with summer rain.

Working the field,
Shadows dancing beneath a murderous sun,
Standing tall like sugar cane,
So hard to be a woman.

Trapped in a surrealist movie,
The man at the bar
Hands me a pen and a paper napkin,
So much depending on seventeen syllables,
Ink unfurling from our wrists
Like sunflower seeds
Ushering in a new dawn,
The moon as black as a rose dipped in tar.

I am in a place where I can write,
Words putting down roots
That we water daily at twilight.

A late burst of birdsong,
The spark that lights the fire.

*Acknowledgements: John Agard, John Keats, Grace Nicholls,
Adrian Spendlow*

Liz Beber

Late Developer
After Marianne Moore

Poetry: I too disliked it.
Couldn't be bothered
with all that fiddle.
Not relevant to me.
Not useful.
I was studying
the important, the intelligible:
calculus, gravitational
vector qualities.
The stuff that makes the world
go round. Quite literally.
No time for things literary.
That was for the kids
with their heads
in the weasel-shaped clouds.
Not for me.
What did a teenager
want with war poets?
But *they* made me.
Shakespeare and Harper Lee;
Owen, Sassoon and Auden
would make me more 'rounded'
apparently. So, I sat on the back
row and rolled my eyes through
the ordeal of 'O' level Lit.
Every English Teacher's
Nemesis.

Forty odd years on and 'rounded'
in more ways than one, I now linger
in my imaginary garden
and feed my ever hungry toads
with Larkin, Frost and Pound.
I've forgotten most of what I learned
of uniform acceleration but the world
continues to spin regardless
while I turn another page. Content
with raw, genuine art. Finally
interested in poetry.

Shirley Bell

My Personal Journey: Poetry and The Open University

What did the OU give me? The music of Yeats,
Ted Hughes and Sylvia Plath, fighting and dying across
the pages, the lush imagery of Dylan Thomas - it did not
feel like course work when I found and rediscovered
the poets with whom I've walked ever since.

The infamous TAD 292 course fired my enthusiasm
in that long ago anarchic week of making and burning
my works of art. Sun and summer in Brighton,
my husband and daughter in a nearby flat, so I stepped in
and out of the study week between my two small worlds.

Back home I wrote a letter to the OU newspaper, in a
desperately seeking poets sort of way, and the
OU Poetry Society crashed and burned into life,
some little fires were lit, and yes, it carried on. Through
TAD292 I wrote my first poems since adolescence.

The imagery from Lean's Lawrence of Arabia,
the manifestation, from dust and distance,
of the ballet stilted legs of the camel, the rider cloaked
in dust and the dark swirl of robes created words
on a page and words and words followed.

The OU Poetry Society was its own oasis in the desert
for me. I wrote, read and discussed poetry. Cassettes
circulated from writer to writer. How much easier then
if we'd had the web. We met from time to time,
face to face, such a hothouse!

And all this has threaded its way throughout
my life. Poetry has been a pain and pleasure.
It has recorded my life, And look, I have grown
so much older. Yet there we are in photographs
from a weekend in Carnforth.

We were so much younger. Poetry was swirling in
the air. It has been my mostly dependable companion
since then for my work has ebbed and flowed,
but my life has always been words on a page,
and words and words to follow.

Mark Bones

But there are blemishes too

With 2020 hindsight,
    now available to all,
must that year forever be
    too painful to recall?
As witless as a ticket to
    the Font-Policeman's Ball?

No doors to mend the pallor
    of a faceless prison wall,
no room for easing thought or limb
    till all expressions pall?
As loveless as a summons to
    the Font-Police~~man~~person's Ball?

Oh spare us, from another year
    of regimented scrawl,
of virulent confinement where
    our friends and poems fall.
As endless as a sentence to
    the Font-Police~~manperson~~offspring's Ball…

Ali Chakir

Mouthing Words

That child
hiding behind curtains and sofas
is me, aged three,
unable to write,
mouthing soft sounds
repeating in patterns,
playing in private with words.
I don't say much when I see people.
I don't like to be seen.
I listen to songs that play in my head.
The tunes are all very simple.
My mother says I'm peculiar.
My father says I'm just shy.
Enough said!
I am neither.
I am learning the scansion of words,
tasting the syllables curves,
and the jolts
the oooh and the aaaah and the hey,
the length of the line and the turn and the stop
and knowing how I should breathe
to express all I'm trying to say.
Every day there is more.
And oh! how it feels,
mouthing the words,
warm as plums, sour cherries,
sharp and tangy,
liquid, looping and round,
spinning oceans and breezes
and trees

with the crack of felled timber,
swinging and splashing
and bathing in wonderful words
that grow deeper and wider and stronger,
and sweet.
They wash me away to kingdoms,
and mountains
and halls full of thunder
and come back to wander in quieter streams
all night in my drifting dreams.

Sally Charnock

Progress...the 21st Century Blues

Between newspapers,
We ate fish with chips,
Swapping coloured sweets,
Buying cherry lips.

Should I see you now,
Would you know my name?
I'd point at politics, laying blame.

I looked for you, and you were gone,
What are the leftovers?
Who now belongs?

Working among a graveyard of typewriters
A silver pen screams uncanny dreams
Signing papers that no one has seen.

Not without some small dishonesty
BREXIT was brought on by democracy,
Covid a nightmare of health bureaucracy,
Immigration, a problem for hypocrisy.
What is the price for this century?
PROGRESS, a solution for modernity.

Cate Cody

Oh You

Oh you opened my view,
released the sound secrets of scholars,
gave me potential voice
as I hoisted modules brick by brick,
shattering, battering,
blowing and growing my mind.

Six studious years toiled;
summers spent tied, yet free
beneath shady trees,
whilst winters prepped and foraged
in forests dense with knowledge.

Children balanced, jobs juggled
as I ploughed through fields
and landscapes muddled
in ologies and the fodder of The Canons.

I quenched in books, scaled
laws of lands, was stranded with
experiments in sound,
and explored unexpected mounds,
perdu où, qui sait
in the past and lasting legacies, (mostly of men).

Then wove that fundamental fibre,
the loss of women;
their worth, work and wonder,
skins of teeth revived, survived.

Boxes opened, unraveled, probed
learning lifelong, so much owed.

Written in homage to the Open University which changed my life.

Phil Craddock

The Lamb, Lamb's Conduit Street – OUP
AGM, Saturday 18th May 1989

As Keith Thompson, Chair, flanked by Buff Monck and Don Allen, the Secretary and the Treasurer, conducted the agenda of the Annual General Meeting, broad rays of sunlight streamed through the sash windows and illuminated thousands of stars of dust.

Seated seemingly randomly around the room, the attendees listened attentively, and as they responded with a comment or a vote on a motion, I gradually became acquainted with the idiosyncrasies of individuals whose poems I had read in the workshop magazine.

Keith took his pipe from his tweed jacket pocket and, after conferring with his accomplices, wound up the meeting. Exchanging pleasantries, we descended to the bar, replenished our refreshments, and returned to experience the performance of guest poet, James Berry.

Necessity had led me to the Open University – to realign my life into a career more certain. But three years of Maths Foundation, Electronics and Computing had channelled a mind requiring broadening. The dust specks danced to the rhythm of James's phrases.

I had managed to gain an Ordinary degree...but this was extraordinary.

Barbara Cumbers

Learning geology
Field trip for S236, Newlands Corner, near Guildford, Surrey

Now that you've seen the landscape
differently, now that you've used its shape,

its vegetation, to feel the bones of it,
now that you've walked from chalk to sand,

from sea floor to rivers to dunes,
you can look at the village

in the valley, at the church
on the lonely hill, the sandpit

carved into woodland, at the way
ridges pale off into the distance,

and know why the grass, the pines,
the vineyards are where they are;

and the land laid out before your eyes
from chalk to chalk is alive

with the changes it's seen
and the stories it can tell you.

Olivia Dawson

On First Reading "The Love Song of J. Alfred Prufrock"
*(The last line is a line taken from
"The Love Song of J. Alfred Prufrock" by T.S. Eliot)*

I fall in love at first sight
with a love song that isn't
a love song – I fall for a lick

of fog, a hint of baldness,
bare arms, a magic lantern.
I'm enticed by words unsaid,

unsettling questions, rhymes
disguised as tricks of the light.
I'm fidgety as a toddler

with a box of coloured bricks, I'm itching
to write a poem of my own,
And how should I begin?

David Dennis

Opalescence

In the last days of autumn
Greybeard leant unsteady
against a hedge of hawthorn,
briar and beech staves.
Old martingale buckle
caught in sheep wool knots
jingle-nailed nativity.
Drizzle-iced winds
blew cep spores
over sedge
where gun-dogs rooted,
sniffing downed feathers.
Crow-wary fieldfares
sought company
from redwings
in berry-strewn stubble.
On a newly oiled gate
some miles off
an owl settled
hiding signs
of past peregrination
with ruffling
and smoothing.
The vole moved.
Greybeard's nose
followed slow
in darkness
along the trudging terminator
not with opal eyes
but sense of smell.

All of this he knew:
the vole's scutter
through sparse clover,
rootless incisors
at next year's meadow edge;
owl in distance, rising.
Then uttering
one disdainful bark,
off again
into the gleam
and crack of night.

Published in Day and Night (Dennis, 2011)

Tim Field

My T.M.A.
With apologies to the Village People

Old man, when are you going to get round
to wearing a graduation day gown,
you'd better sign up and get down
and make it quick and snappy.

Old man, it's never too late
to sample intellectual debate,
so why leave it longer and wait
when you can be so brainy.

But, but, but….

it's hard to write my T.M.A.,
it's not fun writing my T.M.A.,
you can have a tough time
writing free verse and rhyme
it's such a hard thing to do
and I'm telling you
it's hard to write my T.M.A.

Old man, it's a bit of a bind
but grasp it and focus your mind,
you'll soon be feeling just fine
So just get writing,

and when written, that first T.M.A
will set you finding your very own way
to pen an academic essay
and your brain enlightening.

And, and, and......

I've now just written my T.M.A.,
my very own styled T.M.A.,
with poems and prose
and basic typos,
it's such a great thing to do
even if only marked a pass 2
now so proud of my T.M.A.

Kathy Finney

Sandgrown

*An indomitable breed. Their forbears lived along this coast
from ancient times and the blood of many races flows
in their veins – from Sand Grown by Kathleen Eyre (1960)*

I arrived
with the tide
          Mother reeled
me in   between flaccid dunes
and rocks of her nipples   flowing
with brine
as she crooned

Childe I'll tek care of thee.

From the fens of the Fylde
she suckled me
on chats   smoked sprat scraps   collops
in bread   jellied pigs head
swilled down with sluicings
from the Wyre
till my vowels loosened
and Lanky twang
              spilled out
as she chortled

Mother's allus known you were sandgrown.

So I settled
where the Tower steeples above
the sea   ate bait sour
with winkles   potted-shrimp   scratchins
pale-ale.

34

But in the stone-cold foam
near North Pier
the sea murmured
of honeycombed Southern shores
where folk eat tzatziki
in the sun and smash
the dish when they're done.

As the tide washed me
                    away
Mother wiped salt from her eye
and sighed

Go lass an' roam
yo' will never be far from whome
Blackpool runs through thee like rock.

'Sandgrown' was first published in the *Places of Poetry Anthology*
 ed. Andrew McRae (Oneworld, 2020)

M. C. Gardner

journey into the unknown

tired fingers on the laptop
empty music at my desk
in my quiet room, I study,
in my house of bricks
next to the park with ducks
and dog walkers three times a day
in the street by the pond
peppered with electric lamps
shadows of people
engulfed in written tasks
turned into poetic bees
in my tired city with heavy locks
all fluid sleep and taut dreams
pages in heavy books
the water clock strikes midday
it strikes midnight
the chanticleer calls light
on the top of my mountain,
the Muses scramble
to steer my light –
I feel trapped in chaos
sand echoes pebbles,
pebbles echo stones,
stones echo boulders
assessments echo
the bulky horses of history –
under the broken
antique Murano chandelier
I search inside my storm
I can hear empty music I cannot play

I contemplate nebulous mirrors
I select an appropriate task
I am muddled in wicked knots
I journey through the books
ready to begin another revision
the exams? I am on a cliff path
skidding…sliding…forgetting!
a merry-go-round, can I recall
or even understand?
I leap in and out of Black Holes!

Ginette Gibson

My personal journey with the OU

I never put my hand-up when in my class at school
I used to think my classmates would think me such a fool
It carried on at uni, was scared to state my views
Even when they grouped us in groups of threes or twos.
My tutor tried to help me, he tried to start debates
I was too scared to talk though, even with my mates
I left my course at uni, during my third year
Not talking was disabling me, that was really clear.
I worked for years at Membury, in many low paid jobs
One day I thought well blow me, I need to earn more bobs
So I enrolled at uni, I found an OU course
I started out with credits from my old uni of course.
I started with statistics as I felt I lacked the skills
To understand the science and the stats of making pills
I liked the stats so much that choosing the third year
I joined the maths department where there was much less
fear.
I realised I did better at theory than the labs
Preferred to test hypotheses than go out fishing crabs!
I joined the maths OU group, I joined their fun weekend
I started to see that people did want to be my friend
I found I found some purpose, I learnt to talk and smile
I learnt to feel much stronger more confident all the while
I got my course certificate, I passed and all went well
I then went back to hotels for another quite long spell.
I missed so being a student, missed camaraderie
So one day I decided its a masters course for me!
I looked at different courses, most were all online
I felt that the OU course would fit in terms of time.
I chose the mental health course, I got my DSA

I started my first TMA from Feb 17 to May
My tutor was so lovely, she saw what I could do
Even though sometimes I studied on the loo!
The beauty of the OU is you dictate the time
And place where you can study ev'n on the railway line
No early morning meetings tutorials were quite late
I found on OU blackboard my feelings I could state.
I passed my first two modules, I made some OU friends
And then it all went pear-shaped, my strength came to an
                                                    end
And though I've had to defer my project module, see
I know that I'm still part of the OU family.

Julie Anne Gilligan

ARS POETICA: Witness for Posterity

Poet: a scavenger of words, phrases and observations, the gull snatching morsels of credibility from amongst the dross of experience.
Know the rules, then how to break them, make them work for your intention. If they don't then make your own, experiment, espouse invention.

Poetry can unearth, express the extraordinary in ordinary and vice versa,
Become a walking dictionary, words are here to use not bury. Employ syntax to twist and turn, bend it all as necessary.

Linguistic intricacy plus wordplay challenge equals an infinite form of fun.
Humour, wit and irony may play their part for all to see, in language that is understood, not hidden in obscurity.

Poetry can change people, atmosphere, history, attitudes, politics, can give comfort in conflict or disaster, commemorate and witness.
To find a form is liberating, sentence, structure, repetition. Open doors, let more light in on circles, detours, false impressions.

Poetry is the autobiography of an age, written by ghostwriters, a place and time peopled by imagination, illustrated with vignettes and visions.
Ask awkward questions, give answers too, to unasked queries sourced through you. Keep wholly strong, resolute; keep it clear, don't convolute.

Poet: a facilitator, a signpost on a treasure map of many paths, small parcels of metanarrative, that ancient conundrum that fuels philosophers and flummoxes fools.
Nonsense that makes perfect sense, wisdom comes with confidence. From brain to page much dross is lost. Be bold be brave don't count costs.

Remember, nothing is set in stone unless or until it is your epitaph.

Written as part of The Open University MA in Creative Writing, a short version was published in The Hoot
https://thehootstudents.com/poems-about-poetry/ (2019)

Adrian Green

Poetry and The Open University

So many nights
sacrificed
to the curse
of an empty page
and the need to send
those carefully counted words
for assessment
by tomorrow

and when,
against the solemn vow
that it would never come,
tomorrow arrived

the words submitted,
were marked and graded,
then distilled
to a degree certificate.

But yet,
the memory that abides
is discussing Prufrock
in the late night summer bar
and wondering why
the women who would come
and go
talked of Michelangelo.

E. F. Griffin

A PIGGY EXPERIENCE

I met a sow, white with patches,
Once when walking in Wales
And big she was, not to say enormous.
I did not realise pigs could be so large.

But she was glad to see me,
Grunted her approval, pleased,
Not to say delighted by the company.
It is nice to be welcomed even by swine.

Wishing for more than casual friendship
I produced a stale, left-over sandwich –
No, not made of ham, I am not cannibalistic –
From inside my rucksack.

My new found friend recognised it instantly
With that perception peculiar to pigs
As if she had eaten on many occasions
The typical pub product.

She grew wildly excited,
Nearly brought down the fence –
A usual farmer's creation –
In her efforts to grab the food, or me, or both.

In panic I raised the bread,
Threw it far over the beast's head
And, while it was chasing the morsel,
I made my escape.

My friendships always seem to end…
Like this.

Jenny Hamlett

The Weekend
OUP poetry weekend, Chesterfield

It begins before dawn
on a cold November morning

with rain bludgeoning
the north Cornish coast.

The first line of a poem struggles out
as I fight my bicycle over the moor.

Rhythm and metaphor leap
to greet me as I board the train.

Walking towards the hotel
even a duck will start me off.

Embedded in the writing silence
the first complete poem edges into my note book.

Exercise after exercise with poems like bullets
coming too hard and fast to stop.

Words still dance among chats over coffee.
A walk brings on another idea.

Is it possible to drown
under a waterfall of poems?

By Sunday lunchtime
it's time to say goodbye.

I'm exhausted yet
when I slip away

to walk across country,
I pause on a ridge to watch

the smudged outlines of darkening hills
where a Roman army once marched.

I think I hear the tramp of feet,
see flashes of light on helmets and swords

and know for certain
there are more poems coming...

Alice Harrison

Tabula Rasa

The Victorians ruled the lines,
delineated the margins.
With high seriousness
they rhymed their doubts and scepticisms,
hid their deviancies and hypocrisies
in myths and legends or
intricately patterned nonsense.
Believing in their own genius
they penned their great thoughts
in copperplate.

Modernists crossed the lines,
obliterated the margins,
fragmented the surface
with their experiments,
their mixed registers
of allusion and quotation.
Self-consciously individualistic
they shifted their points of view
from corner to corner
with graffiti.

Caribbean writers blurred the lines
with magical realism,
exploded the margins with a scrawl,
sometimes incoherent and illegible,
often fractured by exile and return.
New weaponised symbols
scorched a community's identity.
Their vernacular obliterated tradition

with its own bright, burning
boldface.

With such intriguing, promising stimulation
my page was imprinted.

Lem Ibbotson

My personal journey; poetry and the Open University

Both teacher and student, scientist too,
A lover of verse from my earliest youth
In the OUP I found the chance
To balance my life, and that is the truth

Poetry has helped me to know myself
And to show who I am, for good or ill
I hope that my verses have pleased many
And that the rest do not bear me too much ill will

Sally James

Graduation day (last laugh)

Was it worth it, all those
hours, days, weeks, years,
pouring over books on hot summer days
was it worth all that study?

I can never use it
my degree that is.
Too late now to become
the person I wanted to be.
They said I was a failure
when I was eleven you see.
I remember the tears.

Then on my graduation day
when the black gown was
placed upon my shoulders
I knew it WAS worth it.
It was sheer magic.
I was a graduating granny
with an Open University degree
and no longer a failure.
I remember it vividly.
I could not stop laughing.

P.S. Three years later I got an MA
So now I really am a grandMA

Susan Jarvis Bryant

My Personal Journey: Poetry and The Open University

Beguiled by every wild and wondrous word
That stoked my reveries as pages turned,
I reveled in the wizardry I heard
Till stories in my soul emerged and burned
To light a path to wonders of my own.
A gauntlet from the OU had been thrown.

I took on Byron, Wordsworth, Shelley, Keats,
Blake and his bold tyger, blazing bright,
Iambs, trochees, anapestic beats,
A slew of TMAs that stole the night,
Tricky tomes that tantalized my brain,
And madding crowds that drove my days insane.

I strode with Freud through Mrs. Danvers' head
At Manderley, then swept through Thornfield Hall:
A *Rochester-Rebecca* world of dread;
A torrid, gothic, frolic-littered thrall
That locked me like a damsel in a tower
Scouring books for hour after hour.

I tackled time and gender on a trip
With fair Orlando swathed in Woolfish ways.
I grappled with Miss Havisham and Pip,
Sailed wide Sargasso Sea on Brontë waves.
A spider woman snared me in her kiss.
Electric sheep flocked in my dream's abyss.

I took on Hamlet, Bottom and wee Puck,
King Dick who bid his kingdom for a horse.
With Portia's pluck and just a little luck
I battled through my brutal BA course.
All this to claim the title 'OU Poet' –
I think you'll find these savvy stanzas show it.

Eric Karoulla

Occupational hazard

'What do you do?'
They ask at parties.
I don't know these people,
must I impress or please?

'I write' – I watch their eyebrows
defy the force
of gravity.

'Oh, nothing highbrow…'

Haiku (I like brevity),
sonnets,
couplets, triolets, villanelle.
Rap,
Sapphic verse, -- oh, *c'est belle*!
There was also that long poem that made no sense.
It was so dense, and the stanzas
irregular, lackadaisical –
rhyme's a hazard occupational.

'What do you do?' they ask at parties.
My palms grow sweaty
with the weight of expectation.
Why is my occupation
an endless source of fascination?

'I'm a creative professional,
I got my degree
from the Open University.'

So terse.
But 'I write poetry.' is worse:
they think we speak in verse.

Nigel Kent

Beginnings

Every day at eight o'clock,
although retired,
you'd find me
at my roll-top desk,
seeking to craft
the perfect poems
my partner hoped
would fill the gap
that work had left
but words which were
once my willing workforce,
always eager for employment,
rose reluctantly from bed
and shuffled sleepily
to their stations,
or took a break
without real reason
and sauntered back
at their discretion,
ignoring calls
of inspiration
and when I pressed
them to perform
they'd produce
half-heartedly
a piece of bargain
basement poetry.

Jim Lindop

Portrait of an Old Man

Why have I kept this silver mug with its odd scrolled
                                                handle
and these foxed and crimped-edged snaps of young
                                                people?

And what of this leathery book of names and addresses,
shadows that tempered the relentless sun on unstraight
                                                alleys?

Then there's this ripped-lined, porous pocketed old blazer
that I wore in Budapest after my father died.

Why have I kept these sleek guitars, tacked to the wall
like sporting trophies, where they may chide my failures?

And what of these staid and corporate box-files, swagged
by forty-something years of A4 sheets of ragged poetry?

            But then, there's the music…

What I see when I shave is an old man's baggy head
losing the fixed game with the forces of time and gravity.

There's that self-portrait Rembrandt did as an old man,
when his brushes were still fine and unstiffened…

Rob Lowe

AN END TO SUMMER SCHOOL

That end-of-summer breathing pause
When a whispered something threatens,
When the air is hanging heavy.
Though collectively in amber,
Glowing people rest on benches;
They are talking, drinking, thinking.
They review a year's achieving.

Notice! Fruited trees are tipping
From green to gold to brown, to bare;
And notice! Storm clouds gathering,
As the grass, no longer growing,
Dampens underfoot with lichen.
Notice! Clothed in suits or dresses,
Lightly pressed with linen flowers,
Groomed for smiles or reminiscing,
All ignore their shortened breathing,
Shortened as the days grow shorter.
Notice! How the skin grows colder.
Limbs once young lay frail and older.
Yet notice! As a world goes on,
The universe retains its skin
(Ages pass as slow as marble).
This night skies' frequent shooting stars
Fight the dark of late September,
Illuminating sinewed words
Gathered at many summer schools,
As I relearned the poet's craft -
How to challenge the storm of years.
So notice! In St George's Square

Standing for hope, the right to choose
Sir Harold Wilson's statue whose
University of the Air
Gave breath to everything I dared.

Michael Lyons

An Open University Poet Looks Back Over Forty Years

Forty years ago, nineteen eighty one,
Who knew what would come.
The Falklands War, the Miner's Strike,
Moving to the Isle of Wight.
Deregulation, mortgage inflation, the property boom,
Loads-a-money for some.
The house at Luccombe, overlooking the sea,
But who knew what would come...

Privatisation is all the rage, Building Societies taken over,
Post Offices closing down.
Moving to a flat in Ryde, a change of career.
Nodehill Middle School, becoming poor,
And the head says: "You'll never get rich in teaching."
But who knew what might come...

The nineteen nineties, the Major years
Cash for questions, mad cow disease.
A bigger house and bigger debts,
On Australian dreams the sun sets.
Tony Blair, things can only get better.
But who knew what would come...

The PFI and war after war.
The property boom rolls on
But the bankers, in their greed have been sold a pup,
And the crash sees a run on the banks.
Cobbler Brown to the rescue, but of course,
The weak and the poor must pay,
And we all knew what was to come:

Austerity, no magic money tree,
The roof needs mending, no more lending,
And we're all in this together.
Brexit! What a wheeze! Let's blame it on the foreigners,
There's just one man stands in the way,
Corbyn for peace, justice and equality,
And what came next?

Corbyn's a Communist! a Terrorist! an Anti-semite!
Theresa's too nice,
Boris the joker will soon put paid to Jeremy.
And now we've got Brexit
And a pandemic that's taken too many lives.
But what will come next...

Levelling up? Build back better?
Don't forget that we're all in it together.

Karen Macfarlane

Now I can...
(A mid-life Arts & Humanities student's song)

Now I can read a portrait, wonder why
the lady has a small dog on her bed,
see anger in a stormy summer sky
and labour in a stitch of golden thread.

I know a looted treasure when I see it,
can spot acanthus leaves among the vines,
see power locked in words and how to free it,
and read what's in the space between the lines.

Now I can tap a sonnet, recognise
Antigone when she is in the news,
and hear the child of protest when she cries
out, in the rhythm of a twelve-bar blues.

A heaven-reaching Gothic vault can tell
me sacred stories of the space inside,
and I have watched a poet cast a spell
and reignite a weary nation's pride.

Now I can walk through hidden worlds and see
what used to be invisible to me.

Sam Mansi

Plucking Perfect Plums

Tender words they sing gently.
Plucking perfect plums sensibly
My poetry has progressed
It started off at open mics
A little fun to explore my ptsd

Now plucking perfect plums
Rhyming words for fun
Seems my poetry has progressed.

Culture matters put me forward
They say I could possibly win an award
My poetry isn't that great...
but those plucking perfect plums in sunshine meadows
As I dream away

My poetry journey
Has been fraught
Days of nothing
Sometimes lots.

But here I write
Don't think of those plums
The plucking perfect plums in sunny climes.

This is where my poetry has led me!

Ross McGivern

40:1 (An Anniversary Cento)

Time slips backwards through my fingers
as an old image rises:
taking our chances under blossoming trees.
I had never loved you more
as your lips formed a delicate embouchure
Autumnal kisses taste the best.

Later I knelt in polite perspiration;
a feast for the fasted; an indulgence so sweet
we couldn't help go back for more.
Sweet, seductive Lechery,
now we have eaten our sins
You knew the consequences morally.

Regrets are utterances unspoken,
blanketed bones now rustle the nest.
I chart the contours of our bed
a scent familiar yet foreign.
I don't know why I remember this -
without you, ideas distort time and space.

I whisper *I'm sorry,* erase before.
Darkness washes away your face
and I am now the red stained margin;
the house crumbled on the fen;
a miller grinding shells for flour I'll never knead.
Convulsing in matted air, confused by The Heat
My mouth open, my tongue locked
oh sweetheart come, my sweetheart come.

Lit by memory, moonbeam and flame
she still vibrates, my blood still pools south.
I stir, full of fluid memories
though the last coffee has been supped.
I look down upon an evaporated year:
temptation on the doorstep,
the creak of trunk rub against trunk
temples and tumultuous throbs
Dry limbs, wet eyes, dry heave,
when we came together.

Present and absent
she's here always under my nails
and I am transformed
Think, full stop.

(This poem features one line from forty of my poems to have appeared in the OUP magazine. Where possible, I attempted to maintain a sense of chronological order to give a sense of my OUP journey. However, in order to maintain flow, liberties have been taken)

Hilary Mellon

IN SEARCH OF THE MUSIC

Down countless years they took each other back
And there heard notes once blown inside the wood.
Down countless years beyond that narrow track
To where such songs were known and understood.
As through the rain they followed pipe and drum
Among tall trees and bracken dripping green
To find the reason why they both had come
And taste those notes which clung to lips unseen.

Then, joining past and future in that place,
They took each other on the rain soaked ground
And traced the answers from each other's face
Until they felt the music spilling round.
It poured across his tongue and drowned her cries
In notes which plucked the chord between their eyes.

Published in ODYSSEY Issue 1 – Spring 1990
edited by Derrick Woolf and Steve Davies

published by:
        Pen Press
        Forest Lodge Cottage
        Pen Selwood
        Somerset
        BA9 8LL

Peter Meredith-Smith

WHEN I SET OUT SO MANY YEARS AGO

When I set out so many years ago,
Lacking chart or compass,
In need of a sextant to fix me in my place,
Wanting tools to guide me safe through unfamiliar waters
To a brave new world of better knowing,
I imagined you my lifeboat's sturdy hull,
Holding firm beneath my feet
So I could skip and skim across the waters of the siren seas
Of knowledge and imagination.

You were the vessel of my flight,
In those numbing times of undesired labour:
Work that paid my way but squandered the passing minutes
Of my days throughout those years,
When a young man's dreams were first supressed.

In time I learned I was truly blessed with you,
The ferry of my flight from directionless mundanity.
And as my odyssey progressed my imaginings grew stronger;
Perhaps with the growing of my knowing
Of those things and ways so new and wonderful to me,
Keenly schooled upon the breaking waves
Of an ever swelling sea of learning?

You then became the tiller of my craft of solace;
Holding true my course towards a place unseen,
A place unknown to me until the stitching of the seam
That sealed the sea and sky was split,
Hailing new horizons.

Then you showed yourself the canvas engine of my craft:
The greedy sails of that saviour ship that freighted me
Through time and space to a world of next beginnings.
Greedy sails that gorged on winds of hope;
Winds that came to me in desperate times
To break the doldrums of my wit.

But now I clearly see with hindsight's sharpest eyes
The thing you truly were to me throughout those days.
You were the anchor of my life:
The sturdy grip of an iron fist that held me fast
Through many raging tempests.
You were the guiding hand that kept me true
Throughout the seldom days I languished
In the lulling bays of hinted paradise.

Judi Moore

Shining

I had always known
there was something wrong with me.

At unpredictable intervals
strangely arranged words burst out

which I herded onto pages
hoarded between locked covers.

It wasn't the sort of thing
one could admit to, in those days

when the only good poet
was a dead one.

I thought the activity only useful
for purging, after a relationship broke down

on sleepless nights involving
too much home made wine.

What is a poetry society anyway?
But living poets do exist, like unicorns –

and here, in an intellectually vibrant clearing
they stand: reading, writing, shining.

Vicki Morley

Double Zero Flour

"You can travel fifty thousand miles in America without once tasting a piece of good bread." Henry Miller (December 26, 1891 – June 7, 1980)

San Francisco clocks chime the summer hour.
Rehearsed the route, left powdery footprints right across
sidewalk,

the best double zero flour, weevils will dine well.
My head crusts, breaks through new white shirt.

It crackles, curdles, creaks along my arms,
sparks and conjures the new dawn with static.

Tie, the colour of an electric bruise,
shoes, best soft leather from Siena.

Look, a dangerous eggplant tie reflected
in coffee shop window. Is, a vivid purple, too vibrant?

No, not for a baker — before sunrise
I mix, pound, pummel, stretch, knead, knock the dough,

fill the maws of ever hungry ovens,
feel the heat, jaws of hell, fires of heaven.

Crisp the dough to beautiful bread babies,
ciabatta, focaccia, sour-dough, grissini, pizza, fruit
panettone.

I strut across the piazza, past nail bar
where slinky ladies flutter out to street.

An open window yawns,
a sharp-suited man hollers down to me.

Why it's Antonio. Is he here for the chief baker job too?
Steady, breathe deep and slow, concentrate now.

I'm ready for probing questions,
about flour, yeast, pasta, bread-making, recipes.

Pour espresso, grappa, let's celebrate!
My fruit panettone decided it.

Let's stroll down to Venice Beach,
rinsed by the Pacific Ocean, and swim,

sip cold beers frosting our sticky palms,
sizzle fresh wolf-fish pan-roasted over hot coals,

watch bambini splashing in sea shallows,
while I dream new breads, like a salt-crust San Marino.

Winner of The Plough Poetry Prize 2016

Nigel Pearce

An enchanted odyssey

An ivy house on the hill for those with crooked dreams,
Or so said those anonymous gods in white coats cursing,
Around the wards with the mesmerised floored corridors.
A nurse said, 'you are a no hoper', I was reading Sartre.

Tuesdays and Fridays we were wired to the grid, ECT.
Routine rather than diagnosis, whim rather than science.
My Child Care Order expired, they had to become careful,
Their attitude was transformed, no more jabs or the
                                                  shocks.

Metamorphosis, 'you are clever and creative' Sister & Dr.
'Try the Open University' in 1988, B. As, M. As gained,
Books published; an enchanted odyssey is still my course.
Many did not survive; each death is etched upon my heart.

I stand encapsulated by books, poetry, and prose but alive.

Liz Power

My Road to an Ode

Fear balls like a fist in my stomach
part three of the 'big red book'
how to compose
like wizards of old
conjuring magic words onto the blank page

perfect metaphor, syllable, meter and form
and is it a crime if it doesn't rhyme?
Unwelcome memories surface… 'O' level English
all joy of poetry suffocated
as we analysed the life out of it

leading to certain avoidance.
Now, open the book
start at the start
line by line
my chopped-up prose

finely sliced, diced, discarded
wordsmithery my new obsession
the poem grows
search words to fit, or fit words
explore, play, replace, omit

My first poem turned
out not to be the last.

Kimberley Pulling

Photophilic

Ambition,   says the TV ad.   *It wants*
to Change.   Your.   World.
                                    but was that me?
Was *that* the enzyme scratch in every cell,
that itch of latent biochemistry?

Blanched, sickly rhizome, sugar-starved, I inched
through clay, *itching*, until I stretched one shoot,
one searching tendril, up towards *What if...*
and found it threw a stem, a leaf, a root...

Light opened me in green, pulled me to thrive,
both fed and fuelled a need to grow, to strive
for stronger light, to grow again, to feed -
not from ambition, but organic need.
Earth-blind, I'd had no grand designs for height.
Now, touched, I can't stop reaching for the light.

Rebecca Pyne

On editing a poetry TMA
(for the twenty-seventh time)

The warm study smells of beeswax and pine.
A fondly familiar space – I play
with words, crafting each and every line.
Prospecting, hoping the meter will stay.

Books line the walls. Prose pinned like butterflies.
I wrestle metaphor; polish each phrase –
as classic to modern writers gone by
all show how it's done, repurpose my days.

My calendar keens as it counts down time.
Too short a span 'til the blasted deadline.

Abigail Rowland

On Not Doing Housework at Easter
(for Matilda Jane Ottley 'in service' aged 13)

Here is Matilda, up with the sun, a general reviewing her
troops.
She comes bustling-busy, all fire and disinfectant with
lavender and beeswax on her breath.

Unimpressed, I stay skulking in bed, complaining I can't
see the point.
The point, she says, *is Easter Friday. It's important to get
things done.*

She needs:

brooms and a dust-pan
at least one mop, hot water & two buckets

polish for the furniture
rags for rubbing it in

clean cloths for taking it off
soft cloths for buffing and shining

for the red stone tiles on the scullery floor
half a pint of pink paraffin

Besides all that:

a bar of soap
a proper leather shammy

washing soda, lemon juice
vinegar & Vim

a blue bag for all the nets
gallons of hot water

a dash of Flash and something
strong to get right under the rim.

Matilda liked to pit herself against the stains of winter.
Through gritted teeth and clouds of dust she
would *clean right through* for spring.

Now she runs her finger through my dust.
Have you seen the bloody muck on them curtains?

I'm pleased to see you busy, though.
I like a line that shines as it sings.

Dave Sinclair

Lost in the Ether

After the pub, we eat curry and watch
oddly dressed figures from an exotic academe.
Enrobed in their Levis and 70's wild hair
they dance behind the dust on the TV screen.

We see the thoughts of Euler and Gauss,
appear as lists of poker-faced glyphs
and slowly digest long pondered lemmas
delivered to us via the spells of UHF.

Many years later, the cathode has cooled.
Some memories remain, but mostly they're gone.
The magical echoes of those broadcast thoughts
have faded like the snap of an old popadom.

VHS has departed, as have the folks with wild hair.
But with the theorems they taught, their students propound
the communication protocols
that now send us net bound.

We no longer embrace in the rooms where we met
and Google is now god in our church of the Web.
But teachers still teach and poets still speak,
though sadly I'm now too old for curry before bed.

www.davesinclair.org/poems (2021)

Sue Spiers

The slippery slope and reprobates

It was a challenge to mark the Millennium,
to see if I could, to feel congers in my stomach.
Was I capable, would grey cells mobilize, fire-up?

There was a summer school in Brighton,
a weekend in student halls and taster events –
robotics, civil war history and creative writing.

The author talked of craft, enthused the class
with short stories, flash, poetry. The earthmother
moved us outside to the embrace of trees, hooked me.

I fell in love with the precision of poetry:
language and brevity and forms I could slip
into the doldrums of football on TV, child asleep.

An inch-square advert was almost lost in September
leaflets, a society magazine, outside of assignments –
my first poem in print and strangers' divergent views.

In the dim-lit interior of beer funk and frayed
barstools I held my blue-bound magazine as passport –
was welcomed, kissed, taken as one of their own.

Julie Stamp

Purple

We pushed through rosebay willowherb, tall steeples
of purple loosestrife: delighted in leaving thyme-
infused footprints on grass; in hordes of teasels,

caged and lilac-hazed. We embraced the sublime
grace of sunset: how it haloed single ears of corn,
flooded the fields with warm amber light; subsumed

the glow of naked skin. That evening, he warned
me not to answer back; resolved to needle
like wasps round wine. Clouds gathered and re-formed,

turned amethyst then slate. I knew it was time
to lie low, like violets in shade. After the storm
I noticed tendrils - purple, unperfumed –

twined about my wrists, a posy at my throat:
found flowers from my husband, newly-bloomed.

This poem won the People's Choice award in The Canterbury Poet of the Year awards 2016 and was published in the competitions' anthology and also on Abegail Morely's website https://abegailmorley.wordpress.com/2016/10/24/two-poems-from-julie-stamp/

Polly Stretton

OU Curious Thing

I had a hundred notebooks
some kept 'for rainy days',
I wrote in them at school
in many different ways,
before school, after school,
I left at fifteen,
this was not unusual,
me: naïve, obedient, green.

My parents had expectations.
They bought a shop and obligations:
'For you girls'.
We were schoolgirls.

My notebooks held dreams
and words and dreams
and words and plans for university.
In my perversity:
'Never gonna happen', I said
working in the shop, going off my head.
I married. Worked in the shop.
Children followed. Full stop.

I dreamt university dreams.
One day, ads in magazines:
'Study in your own time'.
Pre-internet, a pantomime.
I phoned the OU.
'Any qualifications?' Few.
Foundation years. Two.

Tutorials and residentials,
I learned to be referential.

Years passed, work intruded, studies fell by the way.
Fallow spell over, soon came graduation day.
A BA with Hons, robes donned
for Betty Boothroyd, who'd been conned
into handing my qualification to me.

Open University opened doors,
and here I am, still with scores
of notebooks to be filled,
words to be distilled
into poems.
Celebrating all these years,
I recall earlier fears
of never getting to write, despite
the hundred notebooks kept 'for rainy days'.

Eve Stripp

Lines on Pages

I look back and see a stranger
I look forward and see a friend
I pause in the moment
Too long and it ends
I see my people
Forever apart
Forever united
Doomed or fated
None still can tell
Not while the pen continues
Lining pages

Julie Stuart

A Taste of Youth

Clicking through teeth   uncrushable
that first startle of a raspberry sour
stabbing my tongue as I sucked   jarring
the soft insides of my cheeks
a puckered calamity of astonishment
piercing blissful through my ridged hard palate

Summer
sends me silent in afternoon's long sunshine
a cold ten pence piece   buried
in my fist
incurring the displeasure of local proprietors
suspicious   in exchange,
then the release of silver
warm as a weapon   hand to hand   the
reassuring impact of a cash register   drawer   ting!

I realised only years later that
lemon sherbets
could pirate my senses in a similar way
shocking my mouth   into life
and sharpening my tongue to clarity

Paul Williams

THIS DAY OF BIRTH I REMEMBER

30 years
$$3 + 0 = 3 \text{ again}$$
12 invites two fifths
      18 wakes on a hangover morning
21 puts puberty to snail trail bed

30 years
$$30/2 = 15$$
scuffed shoes
      trekking him from school
            fiddling with prick in warm spring rain

30 years
$$3 - 0 = 3$$
$$3 + 3 = 6$$
playing on piles of bricks
                  riding bike at road top
suburb
      daisy chain summers
                    home in time for tea

30 years
      ash trays piled in cold flats
memories of white pants girl
under the leaf dropping birch

         I find 6 in a vodka bottle
     15 on a porno mags crumpled page
      18 in the battered face of a lover
         blood dripping from lips
        21 in the cuts on my arms

not by loneliness
nor mist on tarmac road
will I regret
30 years

Rodney Wood

The Advantages of Joining a Poetry Group

An old lady at Summer School thanked
me for reading some crap poems
and introduced me to other writers
who also had no idea what to do with

those precious scraps of paper.
A few months later an ad in Sesame
from Shirley who wanted to start
a poetry group. I thought a chance

to share my work, have it printed,
read other poems, learn to listen
and write critiques, be inspired by
prompts and exercises, write

on a more regular basis and maybe
find an answer to the question
what is it that makes us human,
makes us sing and create?

It turns out the main advantages
are meeting with other poets who want
your company on an immortal journey
pounding a path to Parnassus

or at least something like that.

Kate Young

Open University Summer School, 1985

York, 1985 with nothing but Keats on my mind
I arrived, my arms bundled in dog-eared books
now yellowed with age and riddled with damp;
a far cry from a rental in suburban Kent.

I settled into campus life, admired the lawns
and basked in the sunshine swell of July.
My head was awash with the Romantics,
with notions of love, nature, imagination.

I remember lifting the crumpled page entitled
Mutability, (The Flower that Smiles Today)
by Shelley, my voice a quiver of nerves
skittish as a host of golden daffodils.

I completed the reading aware of his eyes
the colour of amber, flecked with gold
and I spent the week lost in their light
absorbed in sonnets and classical rhyme.

We sung with skylarks, explored Mont Blanc,
recited lines from Songs of Innocence
and by dusk were ready to dance 'til dawn
with the rhythm and swagger of a rap.

It was just as the week drew to a close,
just as my eyes grew accustomed to his light,
that my gaze, now sharp as a crow's beak
landed on the tell-tale sign of another

third finger on the left, a pale-skinned scar
the shape of a lie, a gold band missing.
The flower that smiles today, tomorrow dies.
How subtle the pull of the Romantics.

Final Word – To the Future

Thank you to our current members and to founder members for your contributions to this anthology, all very welcome as we celebrate 40 years of OUP.

Acknowledgements to Julie Anne Gilligan, Activities Officer, for coming up with the idea of a celebratory anthology. Thanks also to Sue Spiers who has edited the many poems you see in these pages. And, of course, my thanks to all of you for sending in your poems, your response has been terrific. I've read every one, some several times. There are 52 poems, one for each week of the year, so there's your challenge, study one poem each week for the next year and perhaps we can have a section in the magazine saying which were your favourites ☺.

I promised you that I'd give a prize from the Archives for my favourite poem, and this has been a dilemma as I reviewed one, then another, then yet another. Finally, it was Kimberley Pulling's 'Photophilic' that became my ultimate choice. Kimberley, expect a small parcel to turn up in due course with a little gift to express my admiration, and thank you for making me smile – this poem resonated with me, we do thrive in full light. I love that you capture the physical / chemical processes in a kinæsthetic way, 'the enzyme scratch…itch' that many will have felt prior to delving into poetry. I like that the poem is uplifting and appreciate so many lines, but especially, ' I stretched one shoot / one searching tendril, up towards *What if...* / and found it threw a stem, a leaf, a root...' and the next stanza's first lines: 'Light opened me in green, pulled me to thrive / both fed and fuelled a need to grow, to strive…' For me, the final line resonates.

Now, what of the future? We've seen so much change over the past couple of years and have navigated it well.

We've had the introduction of 'An Hour or More of Poetry' on the last Thursday of each month, an addition that has been largely welcomed. We'll continue with it as it gives a platform for us all to get together, wherever in the world we may be. Our Annual General Meeting (AGM) last year may have been late but it happened online and was a success, giving many more members the ability to attend, we'll continue to use that platform for future AGMs.

The tutored workshops, also on Zoom, have been sold out for the two years we've run them, another great idea curated by Julie Anne Gilligan. In the future we hope to meet in person for Poetry Weekends at venues in the UK – or maybe further afield, who knows?

Indeed, who knows what the future will bring? Suffice it to say that whatever life throws at us, OUP will continue and thrive with some of the best poets around.

Wishing each and every one of you and the Open University Poetry Society all the best for the next 40 years. It's my privilege and pleasure to Chair the Society and work with our superb Committee and all of you creative poets.

Polly Stretton
Chair
Open University Poetry Society

www.ingramcontent.com/pod-product-compliance
Lightning Source LLC
Chambersburg PA
CBHW060345050426
42449CB00011B/2834